THE GRUMPY GIRL'S GUIDE
TO GETTING INTO COLLEGE

Also by
Rachel Aboukhair

**THE GRUMPY GIRL'S GUIDE
TO GOOD MANNERS**

THE
GRUMPY GIRL'S GUIDE
TO GETTING INTO COLLEGE

by Rachel Aboukhair

New Chapter Publisher
Sarasota 2013

Published by New Chapter Publisher

ISBN 978-1938842-08-5

New Chapter Publisher
23 Osprey Ave.
Suite 102
Sarasota, FL 34236
tel. 941-954-4690
www.newchapterpublisher.com

The Grumpy Girl's Guide to Getting into College
is distributed by Midpoint Trade Books

Printed in the United States of America

Cover design and layout by Shaw Creative
    www.shawcreativegroup.com

Cover photo of the author by Milana Brown

TO DAD

TABLE OF CONTENTS

Cauliflower is nothing but cabbage
with a college education.

—Mark Twain

Prologue

Since the dawn of time, men and women have gazed at the stars and wondered:

Who am I?

Why am I here?

What's my role in this vast universe of ours?

Mighty ponderings of existence which go to the heart of the human condition.

But that is all in the past. Today, such weighty concerns pale in comparison with the one, burning question that torments the minds of American youth—almost to the point of obsession. To wit:

DRRRRRUMMMMMMRRROLL please—

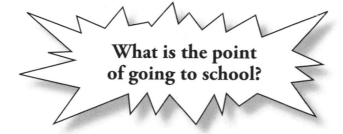

What is the point of going to school?

Is it to obtain knowledge?

Nope.

Get a good education?

Cliché.

Get a better paying job?

No, but good try.

Enjoy the privilege of expanding one's view of the world?

Let's not be silly!

The correct answer, of course, is

TO GET INTO COLLEGE!

And not just any college. It seems a lot of American parents are obsessed with getting their kids into the "right" schools. Some enroll them, as young as three years old, in the "right" preschool or kindergarten, spending upwards of $20,000 a year, just so they will have a better chance of getting into an Ivy League school. I guess, when they ask themselves if their kids can be successful, contributing members of society without having attended Harvard, Yale or Princeton, the answer they hear is, "No, of course not."

So, some of these parents, from preschool on, focus on getting their kids to play the right sports, join the right clubs, do the right extracurricular activities, and finally, get private test-taking lessons so they can ace the SAT, the holy grail of a parent's entire college-preparation process.

Even I knew the importance of the SAT. Indeed, one of my first writing aspirations was an *Ocean's Eleven*-style novel that involved me and a few of my friends breaking into SAT headquarters and disarming it from within. I imagined I was George Clooney planning a heist to retrieve the answer key to help me and my fellow students get a good score. Alas, such dreams are only meant for 30-page, unfinished Word documents and the novel never saw the light of day.

Disappointingly, my parents joined the conformist bandwagon for getting me and my siblings into college and began preparing us with the obligatory high school classes, SAT prep courses, and extra-curricular activities.

Sellouts.

But fortunately, they didn't put emphasis only on college prep stuff. They were also diligent in telling me I'm slouching in public or making me read "self-help" books to cure me of my grumpiness and improve my personality.

Now, my attitude toward college was interesting. I didn't hate college itself (I knew I was definitely going); I just hated the topic, and especially all the *conversations* about it. Why? Well, because most mothers of my high school acquaintances specifically sought out other college-bound teenagers to endlessly grill them—much like TV show scientists with a submarine sonar search for the Loch Ness Monster.

Beep...beep...beep...BOOM! You're trapped!

Now get ready to fake-smile your way through a futile conversation about PSATs and recommendation letters, because all these moms *ever* wanted to talk about is C-O-double L-E-G-E.

From the ninth grade on, I had to endure constant interrogations of what I thought about college.

My conversations with people went something like this:

9TH GRADE

Friend's Mom: *So, Rachel, where do you think you're going to college?*
Me: *I don't know, lady, I'm only 14!*

10TH GRADE

FM: *So, Rachel, what colleges are you looking at?*
Me: *Actually, I'm running away to Europe to become a trapeze artist.*

11TH GRADE

FM: *Rachel, where are you going to college?*
Me: *You know what?—Oxford University!*

12TH GRADE

Someone else: *So, Rachel, have you finally decided–*
Me: *Don't even start with me, Grandma.*

I tried to escape any such conversations because they were tiresome and fruitless. But just between you and me, I was really nervous about all this college talk. What if I'm not smart enough? What if I don't get in?! What if I have to do homeschool college?!? Do they even have homeschool college?

I was distraught for most of my senior year in high school. I just knew I was going to be the joke of the admissions office wherever I applied—a laughing stock! "Hey, Jerry!" the admissions counselor would say, "Come look at this application over here! Rachel Aboukhair? More like Rachel STUPIDkhair. HAHAHA!"

It seemed like the most likely outcome for me.

One day I was feeling particularly pessimistic about the topic and flat-out refused to go run errands with Mom because I told her

I was too busy being grumpy and distraught about my future. She responded by saying that if I'm going to do well in college, I'll have to learn to multitask.

We arrived at the mall. Our entire time there I continued to lament to Mom about the unlikelihood of me getting into college anywhere—until we overheard some college girls at the makeup counter next to us chatting.

"So, where are you from?" the first girl asked.

"I'm from Boston."

"…Boston? Where's that?"

Mom and I looked at each other. That's like saying, "The Atlantic? Where's that?"

The other girl paused and replied, "*Boston*. You know, Massachusetts."

"Oh. Sorry," the first girl said timidly, "I was never very good at geometry."

Mom and I exchanged glances again.

As we left, Mom said that if that girl could get into college, I wouldn't have any problems at all. I was only marginally reassured.

CHAPTER 1

THE RAIN CLOUD
AND A RAY OF SUNSHINE

Before I go into detail about my own adventure journey toward college, I first have to tell you about the cloud. No, not the Internet service—the much more powerful Rachel Aboukhair cloud. For most of my life, I have had a giant rain cloud over my head. Sometimes it seemed close enough to possibly touch my older sister, Sarah, but it would never have the audacity to get her hair wet.

If you read my prior book, *The Grumpy Girl's Guide to Good Manners*, you'll remember that Sarah is Ms. Popularity and the center of the world's attention and I'm Ms. Anti-Personality. If something unexpected happens—regardless of scenario, date, location and persons involved—it usually turns out badly for me and brilliantly for Sarah. So it was at birth, and so it has been until now when I am a sophomore in college and she is a senior.

Except for the time when my mom told us we would no longer be attending private school but would be homeschooling for the foreseeable future.

It was May 27th of 2001, and I still remember Sarah's reaction. "What?!" she cried out.

For the first time *ever*, when the situation took an unexpected turn, it worked out well for me and not for Sarah. I wasn't rejoicing in her despair (siblings never do that—ha!) but rather relishing my own victory (Sarah has had enough victories in her life to override the part of my brain that releases compassion hormones).

At the time of the big newsbreak, we were both going to a private school in Fort Worth, Texas—Sarah having just finished third grade and I having completed first grade. It was on the last day of school, after we'd come home from all of the year-end festivities, and my mom told us both about her homeschooling plan. She had been researching and planning it for a year but didn't tell us, because that's how sneaky people operate.

I was pretty excited; Sarah was devastated. She had 1,001 friends at school, was the center of its universe (yes, even in third grade) and was bawling at the possibility of losing her friends.

If you're acquainted with my mom at all, you know that she is unmoved by tears and hysterics. She had made up her mind, and nothing was going to persuade her otherwise.

She tried to placate Sarah, though, by telling her we would still be friends with everyone and could invite them over to swim and for playdates.

It barely made a dent in Sarah's despair.

So my mom tried a different tactic, "We'll get to travel a lot. We can take fun trips to places and participate in many extra activities we haven't had time for. You'll be able to experience things that would be impossible with a normal school schedule."

Sarah was intrigued but still skeptical. I, on the other hand, was elated. Things were finally looking up for me.

You see, I had not made any friends in kindergarten and first grade. In fact, I had actually made a couple of enemies—even among the teachers. I remember one time my kindergarten homeroom teacher called my mother in for a conference because in the middle of Spanish class I had stopped the lesson and informed the teacher, "You can go home now." I'm sure the reason she got so mad was because I didn't say it in Spanish.

So, I was not losing anything by leaving "regular" school. Actually, I was gaining a great deal. No enemies (yet) and no homeroom teachers to rat me out.

We began homeschooling the beginning of my second-grade year. It was just me and Mom and Sarah. We studied and traveled. We had a flexible schedule and could move ahead in the curriculum. We took trips to New York, Colorado, California and Washington, D.C. We were able to take lots of art and music lessons.

The only disadvantage to homeschooling that I can recall that first year was that there were no snow days. When it snows in Texas, practically the entire state shuts down. Nobody goes anywhere, and the governor calls the Pentagon because he doesn't know what to do when the "fluffy ice" falls from the sky. Well, not really—but almost. It only snows about once every three years, and everybody gets school off for a week. Everybody except us. We were already at school so we had to work anyway.

GGG's Lessons for Surviving the Rain Cloud

❀ Teachers actually like being told to leave. Their outrage is only for show.

❀ A respite from rain may just be the cloud refueling.

❀ Snow is to homeschooling as pleading is to my mother—neither one will get you a reprieve.

CHAPTER 2

MWF School

Well, that first year of homeschooling went so well that Mom decided she was going to stick with it for the long haul. By then, she had met enough people who had homeschooled their children all the way through high school and they had been admitted to good universities. Buoyed by their success stories, Mom set her mind to following in their well-blazed path and making my life experiences as alienating as possible for the sake of homegrown, classical education or whatever.

During the second year of homeschooling (my third grade year), Mom gave birth to my younger brother Michael. He arrived in November, in the middle of the fall semester, but we had to keep learning anyway. So we were forced to get creative with our school environment. We converted one of the upstairs bedrooms into a schoolroom and filled it with baby paraphernalia—bouncy chairs, baby gyms, baby swings, everything necessary for baby Olympics.

There was a distinct disadvantage to homeschooling with the arrival of Michael: When he woke up from a nap, we had to continue to study, and the only way to do that was to entertain him and learn at the same time. Once, when we were studying the capitals of the southern states, Michael started crying. To try to make him stop, I put on a cowboy hat, Sarah stuffed a pillow in her shirt, and together we sang the "state and capital song" for him in a Texan accent. Going from west to east, it went something like, "Sacramento, California; Phoenix, Arizona; Santa Fe, New Mexico; Austin, Texas. Yeehaw!" and so on until we reached Florida. It worked brilliantly. Michael was entertained, we learned the required material, and I called Sarah "Fat Albert" for the rest of the week.

While classes were in session, we covered every subject you would expect for a budding, college-bound third-grader—math, geography, history, spelling, Latin, science. Our minds were also stuffed with grammar rules and grammar drills. I have a distinct memory of the doorbell ringing one day while we were studying some verb tenses. I yelled, "Mom! The doorbell rung!" Of course, this was grammatically incorrect, and she wouldn't let me answer the doorbell until I had properly stated, "The doorbell *rang*." I bet if she found me drowning in the ocean, yelling, "The ship has sank!" she wouldn't rescue me until I said, "The ship has sunk!"

After Michael was born, we didn't go on trips as much, and I missed that. And a year and a half later when Mom got pregnant with John David, my youngest sibling, our traveling came to a screeching halt. I was in fifth grade at that point, and Mom put me and Sarah in an MWF school because she had no energy to teach us during her pregnancy.

Now, what is an MWF school, you might ask? It refers to schools designed for homeschoolers that let you take as many classes as you wish, but they only convene on **Monday**, **Wednesday** and **Friday**, with the parents homeschooling on Tuesday and Thursday—hence MWF school. (Note: There is no short way of saying Monday-Wednesday-Friday school. The only alternative is to say Every-Other-Day school, and that's just as long and cumbersome, so I'm just going to say MWF).

I've been to a couple of these MWF schools, but the one I went to in fifth grade was called "Graeca Academia Puelis et Pueris." If it's not apparent from the name that we sang hymns in Latin every morning, then you are not paying attention. The school was called GAPP for short because saying the full version was worse than saying "Monday-Wednesday-Friday school."

So, when I went somewhere like the hair salon and people asked me where I went to school, I would just say "GAPP."

They would look at me in bewilderment and ask, "The Gap store has a school?!? What do you learn there?!?"

And then I'd have to confess to the nature of the thing, "Oh, no, not the store—GAPP school—you know, Graeca Academia Puelis et Pueris."

And that would clear things up considerably.

Now you may think from the Latin hymn singing that it was a Catholic school, but it was actually Greek Orthodox. A few years back, our friends the Brantleys had started it in their basement, but it grew bigger (the school, not the basement), and so they needed a larger location. A local Greek Orthodox church let them use its building—thus the incorporation of the Greek Orthodox liturgy. The classes were small, and we got a lot of personalized attention. It was mostly like homeschooling, except we had to wear khaki skirts. I don't have anything against khaki skirts as such, but they do convey certain messages to people: "I am a tourist," "I am overenthusiastic about arts and crafts," "I am 10 years old and go to MWF school."

One benefit of GAPP was that the education was super good. The history classes were practically college-level—and we all had meltdowns before each test as if we were really in college. We conjugated Latin verbs and reenacted plays by Shakespeare as a required after-school activity. I was Portia, Brutus' forlorn wife in *Julius Caesar*. Between all that stuff and the khaki skirts, my path towards hip and cool was becoming narrower and narrower.

Anyway, once John David was born, Mom got her energy back and resumed teaching all of us at home, and we left the Gregorian chants behind for the time being.

Mom would teach me and Sarah our lessons, and while we were doing the assigned exercises, she would teach Michael and John David in the adjacent room.

Some of the time the sound would drift from where she was teaching the boys and we could overhear her struggling with the inimitable mind-set of small children.

John David had his own, let's say *unique*, perspective on life. Once, Mom was walking him through a math problem: If there are seven black bears and nine brown bears, that means there are more of which kind of bear? He answered, "Grizzly!"

Another time, Mom, a firm believer in teaching classical tales like *Aesop's Fables*, read him the story of the fox that tried to catch a bunch of grapes hanging high overhead. When he couldn't reach them, the fox said, "They were probably sour anyway."

"What is the moral of the story?" Mom asked John David.

"It means you shouldn't eat any eggplant!" he answered proudly.

Both grapes and eggplants are purple, so maybe that's the connection. Like I said, unique perspective.

But I wouldn't really know. My perspective on things is always accurate.

GGG's Lessons for Surviving GAPP and Aesop's Fables

✿ Everything in my life has been orchestrated to ensure that I become as strange as possible. And it's working.

✿ Let's just move to the Vatican or Mount Athos and get it over with.

✿ Everyone has a different interpretation of classic stories. Don't judge!

CHAPTER 3

WHO IS BRAD PITT?

Unfortunately, like people who wear five-fingered toe shoes, my siblings and I were judged by our peers. Such is the life of all people who bravely journey into the unknown. But, as many a great rapper has said, "Haters gonna hate. They be hatin' on our swag 'cause they can't keep up. Fo' shizzle."

Mom endured some negative societal consequences for homeschooling us, including many a cold, judgmental glance and upturned nose. You see, there is a common misconception that kids taught at home are mentally challenged when it comes to surviving in the "outside world," so to speak. "But what about socialization?" is the tagline on the movie poster of *Horrors of Homeschooling*. The answer was that our "isolation" was abated with homeschool co-ops, sports, church, music lessons and other extracurricular activities. Mom always did her best to answer the scoffers, but they usually clung to their preconceived notions, so she mostly smiled and said things like, "I know, they always squint when they go out in the sunlight."

While Mom merely was being judged, I, on the other hand, was also treated as an object of wonder and thrust into the world of adolescent confusion. When telling a peer of my homeschooling status, a few predictable reactions would follow.

First, they were wondering why I wasn't wearing bulky sandals and a skirt down to my ankles. Then, they felt sorry for me because they thought I didn't know anything about the "real world." They thought homeschoolers were dorky, unhip, unathletic, not permitted to take unsupervised excursions, and only allowed to hold hands with members of the opposite sex after they're married. And that is completely ridiculous—we're *never* allowed to hold hands with the opposite sex.

Usually, when I told my peers that I was homeschooled, they would resort to the "out of touch" stereotype and start asking me if I was aware of anything related to pop culture. Here are two typical questions:

Friend: *Yeah, tonight we're watching American Idol at my house. Do you know what American Idol is, Rachel? It's a singing show—where people sing.*

Another friend: *Rachel, that guy over there kind of looks like Brad Pitt. Brad Pitt's an actor. In movies—movies are like a picture but it moves.*

After a while I stopped fighting and learned to embrace it.

Friend: *I won't be here tomorrow, I'm going to the Switchfoot concert. Rachel, do you know what Switchfoot is? It's a band.*

Me: *A band? You mean like yodeling?*

Despite being treated as a freak show by everyone new who met me, homeschooling did have its advantages. For example, Six Flags has a special day when only homeschoolers can come to the park. I guess even Six Flags thinks we're so awkward that it doesn't want us mingling with its regular customers, but it was okay since I got to spend the day breezing through all the lines because only about 200 people showed up on homeschool day. Ha ha, retribution!

GGG's Lessons for Surviving Public Misconceptions

✿ When in doubt, play dumb.

✿ Dorky is the new swag.

✿ Sunlight gives you freckles anyway.

CHAPTER 4

BIG BROTHER IS WATCHING

As our primary teacher during the elementary years, Mom was fierce—fierce enough to make Tyra Banks proud. Don't get me wrong, I love my mom but—there is no diplomatic way of saying it—she can be…well, terrifying!

It's all very deceptive, really. When you first meet her she doesn't look very scary. She's only five feet tall and weighs about 110 pounds, but do not let her size fool you—she's like the killer bunny in *Monty Python and the Holy Grail.*

One of Sarah's friends, Laena, actually calls her "Mother Gothel"— you know, the scary lady from the movie *Tangled*. One day Laena slipped up and accidentally called my mom "Mother Gothel" to her face. Sarah and I froze, expecting the fire-breathing dragon to emerge. But surprisingly, she thought it was funny and now it's a running joke in our family.

But she really can be lethal. Like one day when my cousin Susan, who lives in Australia, visited us and we were at this restaurant ordering at the counter. My mom was about to hand the checkout girl her credit card to pay for everybody—but my cousin beat her to it and offered her card instead. My mom fixed her eyes threateningly on the checkout girl and said, "*Don't. You. Dare. Run. Her. Credit. Card.*"

The girl behind the counter took a step back, cowered, meekly handed the card to my cousin and said, "That's the scariest look anybody's ever given me."

And that was with a total stranger. Imagine what she was capable of if her own kids strayed!

On top of that, she always found out about everything we did. Everything! I'm almost certain that she had a network of spies set up around the country consisting of moms, teachers and Orcs that made sure anything her children did got back to her.

Once I skipped Bible study to go to Starbucks with my friend Melissa, and when I walked into our house Mom was sitting in an armchair in a dimly lit room with her back to me. She spun around stroking a fluffy, white cat in her lap and asked, "So, how was Starbucks?" (I might be taking poetic license with the cat because she never let us bring animals into the house, but you get the idea.)

I don't know which was worse: the fact that she always knew about everything almost before we did it, or that we could never get away with it.

One summer, my mom found out about some behavior on Sarah's part that she cryptically called "disobedience." I never discovered what it was, but Mom had Sarah's cell phone disconnected, took away her car, cut up her credit card, confiscated her computer and forbade her from seeing or talking to any and all members of humanity for six weeks. ***Six weeks!***

Sarah kept asking her how she found out about the aforementioned "disobedience," but Mom wouldn't say. It confirmed all of our paranoid conspiracy theories and established as a fact of our existence that

BIG BROTHER IS WATCHING YOU!

If ever my mom got lax and didn't monitor us like the NSA, I *still* couldn't get away with anything because everyone, but *everyone*, knew my dad, who is an Ob-Gyn and has delivered practically everyone's babies in our part of town.

The conversation generally went like this:

Random Lady: *Rachel Aboukhair? Are you by chance related to Dr. Aboukhair?*

Me: *That I am.*

Random Lady: *Oh, he delivered my twin girls!*

Me: *How nice for you.*

Or perhaps:

Random Dude: *Do you by any chance know a Nab—what was it—Noble?*

Me: *Nabil Aboukhair*

Random Dude: *Yes! Nabil Aboukhair!*

Me: *Never heard of him.*

One day I was driving home from my flute lesson and I got in a minor traffic accident. The couple whose bumper I hit on the freeway was from New York. After we pulled over to the side of the road, we were showing each other our IDs when the guy read my last name, looked up excitedly and asked if I was related to Dr. Aboukhair.

Oh, come on, that's ridiculous! You're from NEW YORK!

"Yes, he's my dad."

"Oh my gosh, that's so funny! You know, he delivered my first daughter before we moved to New York!"

"Of course he did."

The police officer arrived in due time (hitting somebody's bumper isn't that big of a deal, yo!), and the New York guy told him animatedly, as if he'd sighted a celebrity, "Officer, you know, her father delivered my first child!"

The policeman blinked and said, "Huh, small world."

How droll.

I am sooooo getting out of this town.

GGG's Lessons for Surviving Living in Your Hometown

❀ Never lie about your whereabouts—either Mom or one of Dad's patients will find you out.

❀ You still have to pay for car damages even when your dad delivered the guy's baby.

❀ Mom's fierceness decreases only 3% around strangers.

CHAPTER 5

ANCIENT HISTORY

The biggest advantage of homeschooling (other than the Six Flags thing) was that I was able to care less about my appearance than I normally do since there was never anyone around to see me. I usually wore my old jeans and two different kinds of Hello Kitty socks with my hair in a ponytail, accessorized with a headband and a banana clip—all at the same time. As you can see, all those months attending the "GAP" school really paid off. Not to fear, Sarah always reminded me that there was no lower rung for hair shamelessness than a headband and ponytail worn simultaneously.

A typical homeschool day would start out with me waking up at 8 a.m. and dragging myself to the kitchen and getting breakfast. After I poured myself some cereal, Mom would begin our day with a lecture about ancient history and how relevant it is to our everyday lives.

Then, inevitably, Michael and John David would escape from our housekeeper, who was taking care of them, barge into the room and say they wanted to play. So, when we took a break for a snack or something, I would be a good sister and indulge their youthful imagination in a menagerie of make-believe. I know, you're going to say, how noble of you, Rachel! But their childish innocence was terribly misleading and dangerous to my existence. John David liked to climb on a high surface like the kitchen counter, jump on my shoulders and then slide down my head in what felt like an attempt to snap my neck. As I stumbled to the floor, Michael, two years older, displayed his burgeoning Mixed Martial Arts prowess and tried to jump on my stomach. I, helpless and alone, could only shield my ribcage with my legs as his nine-year-old boy body slammed into my diaphragm and other equally vital organs.

I ended up fending both of them off with couch cushions and then running into the laundry room and hiding behind our housekeeper until Mom would finally interfere and call our wrestling match a draw.

But back to ancient history. For some reason, this subject really excited my mom. In the early years, she had us reading Josephus, a Jewish Roman scholar who witnessed the destruction of Jerusalem, and later she moved on to Plutarch and Arrian, who chronicled the military exploits of Alexander the Great. How this would help us get into college wasn't clear to me then (or now).

One of her favorites, though, was the Code of Hammurabi. This was an ancient set of laws by Hammurabi, a Babylonian king. It is important because it is the oldest existing law code, providing the earliest rules of justice for women and slaves (which apparently was unusual throughout the ages), standardizing contracts, regulating private conduct, imposing penalties and stuff like that. JUST LIKE MY MOM!

There are almost 300 of these laws, preserved on stone tablets in a language no one speaks anymore.

Some of them simultaneously make a lot of sense and no sense at all, if that makes any sense. A lot of them go something like this:

> *If anyone bring an accusation against a man, and the accused go to the river and leap into the river, if he sink in the river his accuser shall take possession of his house.*

It could just be me, but I bet many a person who was coveting his neighbor's house took advantage of this one.

Here's another:

> *If a builder build a house for someone, and does not construct it properly, and the house which he built fall in and kill its owner, then that builder shall be put to death.*

I guess good ol' Hammurabi didn't know that the greatest punishment—as my mom likes to say—is knowing you didn't do your best work. He had to take it a step further.

It seemed to me that his laws were pretty extreme, but the more I thought about them, the more I realized they weren't all that bad. And they gave me ideas for some of my very own to regulate the conduct of some people I know.

How about:

> *If your cousin borrows your car and brings it back and has changed all of your saved radio settings to classic rock stations, he shall be cast in the river with a stone around his neck—Jeremy!*

Here's another good one:

> *If your Aunt Mona knocks over her coffee mug and said coffee spills onto your brand new MacBook Pro and fries it, such aunt shall be tied up naked, covered in honey, and tossed onto a mound of fire ants.*

Whoever said ancient history isn't relevant to our times? If they ever make me king, I'll have to pass these along.

GGG's Lessons for Surviving Ancient History and Your Brothers

✿ Never wear a ponytail, headband and banana clip simultaneously.

✿ When attacked by children, assume the "cannonball" position: curl up, face down, wrap hands around your legs.

✿ Remember to complain less frequently about Mom's punishments, since they are often less outrageous than Hammurabi's.

CHAPTER 6

TRAGEDIES—GREEK AND OTHERWISE

Besides history, Mom also loved literature. She actually loved all books, including books about grammar and grammar about books—because, I'm assuming, she was always picked last in kickball as a child. When we were in high school, she loved making us read ancient Greek plays like *The Eumenides, Antigone, Oedipus the King*, and books with equally unattractive, tragically-named characters.

I actually did enjoy these readings. I liked the various aspects of Greek plays—the furies, unavoidable fate, the tragedies. They seemed written for me! But, of course, I could never let Mom know that I enjoyed them, so when she asked us, "Did you guys understand the Sophocles reading?" I said, "I don't know, it was all GREEK to me! *Hahaha!*"

She neither laughed nor commented because she only responds to my unstupid comments.

For reading on our own, Mom said we could choose whatever we wanted, not counting *The Chronicles of Prydain*, anything by Lemony Snicket or "anime" books—"basically, all the weird things that Rachel likes to read." I started to protest but knew better, so I chose *Crime and Punishment* because the title seemed to mirror the direction I felt my life was going at the moment. How can you not enjoy Russian literature? It's so uplifting. And long! And confusing. Each character has about six different names, and I managed to catch on after about the first 400 pages. But I jest. Actually, I did enjoy it, maybe because everybody always dies at the end.

The author of Crime and Punishment
in one of his lighter moments

You'd think that being homeschooled—and doing all the stuff Mom made us do—we would at least be free from homework. But *noooooooooo*. Not only did we have to sit with Mom all day and learn all kinds of unusual lessons, but she also gave us homework to do all evening.

"Technically, it's not homework," she'd say disingenuously, "because you're already at home to begin with. *Ahahahaha!*"

I could only see that comment as sadistic.

When my dad came home from work, I tried to complain to him. But he had this habit of always trying to one-up me by having a better story of suffering. So when I started to grumble about being stuck at home, having to do homework or lament that pajamas stop being comfortable after you wear them for eight hours straight, he would start in with this long story about when he was a kid and had to wake up at 5 a.m. and walk to school in the snow with no shoes and no socks. Uphill both ways. Then, when he got home, if he wanted dinner, he had to go out and catch a goat, kill it and cook it himself. "Oh yeah? Well…I have to…to…read Greek plays…!!!"

That didn't really work, so I went upstairs and opened my book and cheered myself up with *Crime and Punishment.*

I later found some pictures of my dad when he was a child, and he did *so* have socks and shoes. He had an Afro too, but that's for another book.

GGG's Lessons for Surviving Your Dad and Ancient Literature

❖ Learn to embrace the Greek tragedies—since they tend to mirror my life most of the time.

❖ Most things are Greek to me.

❖ Old pictures of your dad's Afro can and will be used as blackmail.

CHAPTER 7

STEPPING OUT

Dad is actually a pretty cool guy, but if ever I had plans that involved a boy, he freaked out and the event was off limits.

I distinctly remember one Thursday night while I was in middle school, my friend Ashley invited me to go to a Foo Fighters concert with her and her two older brothers. I asked Mom if I could go and she told me to ask my dad.

Me: *Dad, can I go to a concert tonight?*
Dad: *What concert?*
Me: *The Foo Fighters.*
Dad: *Foo who?*
Me: *Foo Fighters.*
Dad: *What's that?*
Me: *It's a band.*
Dad: *Oh. By yourself?*
Me: *No, Dad! With Ashley and some other people.*
Dad: *What other people?*
Me: *Her brothers—*
Dad: *BOYS???*

Me: *Yeah, Dad. Boys.*

Dad: *You cannot be with boys unless you are married to them!*

And that's the way it went. Usually anything I wanted to do didn't slide with Dad's #1 house rule: no being around boys until you're married. And maybe not even then.

"So after I'm married, then I can date everyone I want?"

"Ye–No! Just your husband!"

That night was pretty interesting. Instead of the Foo Fighters concert, I hid behind my desk and jumped up and scared my betta fish, but then I felt bad about doing that and cleaned his bowl as compensation.

GGG's Lessons for Surviving Being Stuck at Home

✿ **Make sure all of your male friends have girl names (e.g., Kelsey, Ashley, Stacy) or you'll be home all night playing with your imaginary friends, Tania and Zeus.**

✿ **You cannot be with boys unless you're married to them, but I'm sure that speaks for itself.**

✿ **Fish have a short lifespan anyway.**

CHAPTER 8

MUSIC TO MY EARS

My mom supplemented our homeschool education with various music lessons. She wasn't musical herself but thought playing an instrument was important. Since we were going to apply to college as homeschoolers, she said we had to have a varied background, filled with different accomplishments, so to speak. It sounds reasonable enough, but the torture of music lessons was not to be limited to one instrument. We had lessons for the flute, guitar, piano and drums. I was never any good at any of them so I always behaved badly with the teachers. I'd become lethargic, passive-aggressive, and then mean—progressively and in that order.

Like with my guitar teacher, Josh, when I was nine.

As he was teaching me chords in one of our lessons, I suddenly said, "That was really funny."

"What was funny?"

"That part in the movie *Remember the Titans* when they do the dance before the football game."

"…When in our conversation today did we bring up *Remember the Titans?*"

"Oh, you don't recall that?"

Of course, we never did discuss the movie, but I introduced self-doubt into his world, which made it a successful day for me. I set the pattern with him and it became a kind of addiction with me toward all subsequent music teachers.

For some reason, my piano teacher Eddie was the only music teacher who didn't run away from our house, screaming for his life. But maybe I'm being too hard on myself. The first guitar teacher didn't run away screaming either, he just snuck quietly out the back door, never to return. And the previous piano teacher said he was "moving to Africa" to "work with the natives." I wonder if that's code for seeking treatment at a mental institution.

Anyway, Eddie stuck it out until I was 18 (which was the age Mom said I could quit piano), and he was pretty cool all the years I took lessons with him.

One day when he began teaching me a new song and I came to the bridge where I used the soft pedal and played it slowly, he said, "Slower."

I played it slower.

"Even slower than that."

I played it even slower.

"Still too fast. Play it very, very slowly. There is no such thing as too slow for this passage."

So, all week, I practiced it slooooowwwwly.

The following lesson, when I began to play the bridge, he said, "It's too slow."

"What?! You said there was no such thing as too slow for this piece!"

"Yeah, I changed my mind. Now it just drags on."

And *this* is why in the movies the adults can never fix anything.

Eddie also made us participate in biannual piano recitals that he held for all of his students. Actually, it was my mom who made me do them, but that's beside the point. I detested these recitals. Dreaded them. I mentally prepared myself *months* in advance for the nervous breakdown I planned to have the day of the actual performance. I don't actually know what being chased by a man wielding an ax feels like, but I believe it is very similar to the feelings I had right before I went up and performed in front of 30 people at The Club for Old People downtown.

Okay, that's a bit inaccurate—it's actually The Club for Old *Women*. That's where the last few recitals were held, and the place I tried to avoid two Saturdays a year at 2 p.m.

Before I could drive, I would try to hide in various spots inside my house, but I never had the courage to actually *run away* from my house. An important rule to learn, kids, is that the temporary pain of a piano recital is a lot better than the eternal pain associated with your face being physically removed from your head (which is what my mom threatened to do if I ever ran away from home).

Sometimes on the way to the recital I would mentally come up with different schemes that would get me out of the piano recital. Maybe I'll "lose" my sheet music before I get there? Nope, I've heard other students tell Eddie that at the recital and he said, "Just do your best to play it from memory." If I ever had to play a piece from memory I'd probably have a stroke. Hey, maybe if I play very horribly, Eddie will ask me not to do recitals anymore, and I'm free! Fat chance. That would not deter Mom. She would probably request he have a separate recital just for me and invite total strangers to attend with the promise of free cookies.

One time during my performance, I actually zoned out during the song and "woke up" in the middle of it and wasn't sure where I was. I panicked, fumbling and messing up, before I found my place in the score. I remember thinking, "It'd be really nice if a car drove through the wall of this building right now." In fact, all my fantasies of freak disasters coordinated exactly to the times I had to play at piano recitals—but don't worry, the fantasies only lasted a short while and nobody actually got hurt except the piano.

And if it weren't bad enough that I was no good at piano, I was even worse at guitar. Sarah took lessons with me, and I know you're shocked to hear that she was excellent at playing guitar (and the piano). In fact, she became a musician and even wrote her own songs, which she recorded. Check her out on iTunes.

Anyway, our guitar teacher, Dave, had a son who was in a local band. Sarah was obsessed with his band. So she asked Dave if he would have his son take one of the band's posters she had on her wall and get the whole band to sign it. Dave said, "Sure," and then asked me how to spell my name. I figured he meant my last name because 1) who doesn't know how to spell Rachel and 2) everybody always asks me how to spell my last name—so I said, "A, b, o, u, k, h, a, i, r," while he wrote it down.

When his son took the poster to the next band practice, one of the other band members, as he was about to sign it, asked, "So there's Sarah...and Aboukhair?"

"Yep."

"Aboukhair? Did she get in trouble while they were naming her or something? Why would they name her *that*?"

He shrugged. "I don't know."

So when Dave brought us the poster the next time we had guitar lessons, underneath the picture of the band were their signatures with the words, "We love Sarah and Aboukhair!"

At first, when Sarah and I looked at it, we thought they meant to write, "We love Sarah Aboukhair," but somehow an "and" got in the way. Or maybe they loved her so much that they loved not only Sarah but also Aboukhair. Two things we love! So we looked at Dave and asked him why it said Sarah AND Aboukhair—and it finally dawned on him that my name is Rachel and not Aboukhair—and he told us the story that he and the band had thought my name was Aboukhair.

See what I mean about the dark cloud?

If piano and guitar weren't enough to include on our college resumes, Mom also made us take flute and drum lessons. As I said— *enthusiastic*! My flute teacher was good and no-nonsense, so I didn't dare misbehave around her, but, for some reason, my brain ceased to function around the drum teacher.

I won't mention our drum teacher's name to avoid causing him any more trauma than I already have, so let's just call him Bob. He had long black hair and glasses, and was really cool—just what you would expect from a drummer.

Sounds good, right?

But since we don't live in an alternate universe where I'm normal, I made sure the situation went downhill before he could say "this kid is a pathological weirdo." I became super bad super fast and I'm sure he was pretty close to paying me *not* to take lessons anymore. He would ask me to play something, and I would act like he never spoke and just sit there, a lifeless, listless form. When I did speak, it was to say something rude. And I was only 11 at the time.

He kept asking my mom what was wrong with me and why I was so mean to him. Of course, she had no answers, as I was a mystery to her as well. She apologized profusely and often, but when my behavior did not materially change, my mom decided to end his misery and terminate my drum career. Success!

But then one day I found out Mom invited him over to lunch to apologize to him once more for my behavior. She made me say hi to him as I was sneaking out the back door trying to avoid him. After I managed a forced greeting, I withdrew to the backyard with a sandwich and stayed outside the whole time he was there. Why didn't I stay at the kitchen table and ruin lunch for him? I guess because my primary work was done, and one of my most important mottos is "Quit while you're ahead" (right next to "Never trust anyone who wears non-utilitarian glasses").

GGG's Lessons for Surviving Music Lessons

✿ Consider the fact that I might be the reason musicians have a reputation for being strange.

✿ Faking a stroke to get out of a recital will not prove successful. Your mom will make you give a piano performance in the ICU.

✿ Look up local mental institutions and see if you can find one of your ex-music teachers there. You owe it to them to visit once in a while.

CHAPTER 9

UNSPORTSMANLIKE CONDUCT

In her ever-expanding endeavors to make the college resume well-rounded, Mom decided to add sports to the daily activities. But she never dared put me in organized sports because she feared for the safety of the other team members. That, in effect, eliminated basketball, volleyball, soccer, field hockey and softball from the list of possibilities because all of those sports required me to cooperate with someone.

So she decided to send Sarah and me to karate and tennis lessons, since those can primarily be done solo. There was a clear dividing line between my sister and me when it came to athletic activities—Sarah was passive and I was aggressive. When a tennis ball flew past her, she'd let out a feminine scream and six guys would run to get the ball for her. I, on the other hand, affected a bored look until the ball came near me, and then I swung at it so hard the instructor had to duck.

The tennis pro tried to be diplomatic, so he commented, "Sarah, you have good form; we just want a little more intensity. And

Rachel, um, I like your strength, but just try not to aim the ball at my head, OK?"

I ended up quitting tennis as soon as Mom let me because I lacked skill, coordination, accuracy and grace. Other than that, I was really good at it. Even though lessons were officially over a long time ago, I still "play" tennis from time to time when we go on vacation. I've learned to add a Rafael Nadal grunt to every movement, as it considerably distracts people from my lack of skill. Try it sometime. It works.

Karate was just as "fun" as tennis, and once again Sarah and I displayed our respective approaches.

Our instructor showed Sarah some self-defense methods to use when people try to mug you or stab you or punch you.

"So, if someone comes at you with a knife like this…"

Sarah, horrified, cupped her face with her hands, "Why would someone come at me with a knife?!?!"

"If they wanted to stab you."

"What?!?! Why would anybody want to do that?!?!"

Then it was my turn. The instructor held a punching bag and told me to kick it as she walked with it backwards.

"OK, good, good, a little higher, good, OW! Watch my fingers! OK, stop!"

The highest I got was a yellow belt with a green stripe.

So watch out.

GGG's Lessons for Surviving Sports

✿ Sports are a way to express yourself. That's why I have been banned from most of them.

✿ Apparently, "try your hardest" is the one edict athletic teachers want me to avoid.

✿ Running around after a little, yellow ball, especially when grunting like Rafa, is undignified anyway.

Chapter 10

College Role Models?

During all this hysteria of preparing me for college, my cousin Paul came to visit us one day. Paul was a freshman at Baylor University in Waco, which is about an hour's drive from our home, and, of course, Mom tried to tie his visit to the topic of college. She talked to me beforehand to convince me to ask him questions about applications, interviews, SATs and so forth. "That way you can get a head start in ideas and approaches," she said.

I was excited to see Paul. He was always doing something odd, but you never could tell if he was doing it on purpose or if he didn't know how bizarre it was. For example, he wore flip-flops, wrinkled plaid shorts and flannel shirts to church and looked all bewildered when you asked him why he was wearing that. For about a year, he sported a weird hairstyle that looked like he had just entered a chia pet look-alike contest…and won. Lately, he had been growing his hair out because he wanted to get dreadlocks. He didn't get why having a hairstyle that allows you not to wash it is gross.

On this particular occasion, he called us to say that he was running late because he had just gotten out of a student leadership meeting with the president of Baylor. My mom was impressed. She couldn't wait to hear about it.

When Paul showed up at our house, he was wearing maroon Dr. Pepper pajama pants and a blue t-shirt.

"Oh, you went home and changed before you came over?" my mom asked, surprised.

"No, I came straight from school."

Mom's eyebrow twitched. "Uh, no, I mean, after your meeting with the *president*, you changed and then came over here?"

"No, I went to my meeting wearing this."

"You met with the *president of Baylor University* wearing *Dr. Pepper PAJAMA pants*?"

"Yeah. Laundry."

For once in my life, it was someone else who acted like a dork and was the recipient of Mom's mortified glare. I welcomed the much-needed break.

In an attempt to mask her extreme annoyance, Mom tried to change the subject by asking about his brother. "Where's Jeremy? I thought he was coming with you."

"Oh, he's not coming. He broke his arm."

"Oh, no!!! What happened?!"

"Well, Jeremy's friend got in his car to leave school and Jeremy got the idea to run up on the hood of the car and then lie on the roof. His friend took off and Jeremy flew off the hood and broke his arm."

Eye twitch again.

I chimed in. "Well, at least he wasn't wearing Dr. Pepper pajamas when he did it."

My mom left us alone—probably because she had reached her

limit of eye twitches for the day—and also to give me time to ask him some advice about getting into college. He was super helpful. When I asked him about SAT-taking strategies, he said he never studied for the SAT—he just showed up the day of the test and took it. When I asked him why he chose to go to Baylor, he replied that it was the only college around here that didn't require an entrance essay. I could see that his advice was going to be invaluable and therefore ceased all further questioning. He did say, however, that for fun in Waco, he and his friends go to the bridge over the Brazos River and throw tortillas at the bridge columns. Uh-huh.

GGG's Lessons for Surviving Your Cousins

✿ You can totally judge a book by its cover.

✿ If the cover reads "Dr. Pepper merchandise," don't touch it or look at it.

✿ Stupid accidents are always comical if you just roll your eyes and say, "Boys will be boys."

CHAPTER 11

EUROPE, LOOK OUT!

When the boys grew a little older, Mom decided we could start traveling again. At this point, Sarah was in 10th grade, and I was in 8th. My brothers weren't much older, by the way, only three and five. I was aghast that Mom wanted to take them on international trips, but she said she didn't want to delay anymore because she thought going abroad was educational and would also make good topics for college essays. Oh, boy, would it.

The first such trip with the boys was to France. Sarah wanted to go to this summer program in Paris to study the language and French literature. The program was only a month long but Mom wouldn't let her go to Paris alone at that age, so she decided that she and the rest of us kids would come along, rent an apartment close to where Sarah's program took place, and check in on her every few days.

Like I said, "Big Brother."

Dad was going to be with us for the first week to help us get settled. Then he'd fly back to Texas and return to Paris at the end of the month to take the boys home. We girls would stay and continue on to

Switzerland and Italy with our friends the Harrisons from Fort Worth, who would meet us in Paris at the end of the month.

When we started packing, Mom had each one of us put six jars of peanut butter in our suitcases. For some reason she was convinced that there was no peanut butter to be had in all the sovereign state of France.

She said, "We must always prepare for the worst."

That is when I realized how privileged we were. If the worst-case scenario was being stuck in France without peanut butter for a month, well then we were going to be fine. This is what I thought as I reluctantly packed them into my suitcase—until I read the label. I was packing six jars of *organic* peanut butter into my bag. Organic peanut butter—the kind that you have to stir because the natural oils settle on the top. Then I realized that the worst-case scenario was being stuck in France *with organic* peanut butter in each of our 12 suitcases for a month. My next thought was, *Oh, well, I just hope that bringing 72 jars of organic peanut butter into France isn't cause for deportation.*

Considering how the first week unfolded, I would have actually preferred deportation. The initial plan was for Michael and John David to attend a French preschool in the mornings while Mom and I went sightseeing and visited museums. Then we would pick them up in the afternoon and spend the rest of the day with them. It seemed like a reasonable enough plan.

But remember the dark cloud? You see, John David was three and not yet toilet-trained. That is normal in America but apparently not in

France. It made my mom the poster child in Paris for how *not* to parent. The preschool would not take a child who was not potty-trained, and when my mom insisted that no one had mentioned this to her when she had called ahead to sign up the boys, the female administrator said in English with a French accent out of *Madeline*, "I did not *dreeeaaammm* zat a *zrree*-year-old would not be trained on ze toilet!!"

The administrator relented enough to say she would leave it up to the individual teacher of John David's class to decide, but when we went to the classroom, the teacher (who happened to be American) balked. Living in France must have rubbed off on her, because she said in a nasal, pompous voice, "I, as an educator, do not change diapers."

This, as *20 toddlers* ran around the room screaming. I don't know what kind of "educating" she thought she was doing with them.

I was about to chime in with my own snippy remark, when Mom said, "That's fine, don't worry about it," and walked out.

WHAT?! Don't worry about it!?! We weren't just going to take that lying down!!

But it was over. They wouldn't take John David, and Mom wasn't going to create a fight or leave Michael there without his brother, and so the boys joined us everywhere we went. I finally knew what Charles Dickens meant when he wrote in *A Tale of Two Cities*, "It was the best of times, it was the worst of times." We were in Paris, the City of Lights, the most romantic place in the world—babysitting two toddlers, one of whom wasn't potty-trained.

They always felt cooped up and restricted because much of what there is to do in Paris is indoors. They were so bad that one day a taxi driver yelled at my mom and said, "Who is in charge here?!?! You or them?!?!" Them.

For some reason, the boys woke up every morning at 5 a.m., just around the time Mom was starting to drift off. (I guess the stress didn't let her fall asleep earlier). She would let them watch French cartoons when they woke up so she could sleep a little in the morning. I usually slept until noon.

After that, Mom always planned for us to go on excursions, usually in the name of having "valuable educational experiences." She dragged us to museums, galleries, old churches, Monet's home, castles and even Euro Disney; but at the end of the day, we always ended up at a children's park we found in the Luxembourg Gardens.

The place was beautiful and enchanting and filled with amazing sculptures, verdant gardens, ponds and walking trails.

In one corner, near Sarah's school actually, was a cool playground with jungle gyms, slides, swings and the like. We went there at the end of almost every day because what else can you do with two, um, energetic boys in the middle of Paris? They could handle the museums only for so long.

While they played in the park, I studied my European map to find an escape route from Paris to Texas. But invariably that darned Atlantic Ocean got in the way of any plan I conceived.

To avoid going totally insane, Mom made Sarah leave her Francophile friends from school every weekend and come stay at the apartment to give us a break from the boys. The minute she arrived, Mom and I took off as fast as we could—to the farthest tourist attraction from our apartment possible without actually leaving the city of Paris. We didn't return until we were sure the boys were asleep for the night.

The reprieve was always too short, and I counted the days on the calendar until Dad would return—sometimes I went over the calendar five or six times a day—hoping I had messed up the countdown and that Dad was coming back sooner than I thought.

We were constantly overwhelmed with the boys, so I don't remember much about the "valuable educational experiences." One thing I did observe while we were in France is that they didn't offer you ice in restaurants. Apparently, ice does not exist in Europe. When the waiters brought our drinks, they were often at room temperature. When we asked for ice, they gave us the same look the preschool administrator wore when she heard a three-year-old was still in diapers.

It wasn't any real inconvenience, and when we returned home I had another card in my pretentious snob play deck. "Oh, *ice*, how droll! It has been so long since I partook in such decadence; you know, in *Paris*, they don't use ice, but I will condescend just this once and indulge in some."

By the time Dad arrived to take the boys back home with him, we had barely managed to survive. Dad couldn't understand why Mom and I looked so stressed. Later, I found out that the boys kept vomiting on the whole flight back to Texas, and I was secretly happy because Dad got a small taste of what Mom and I had suffered for an entire month with the dynamic duo.

With the boys finally gone, Sarah, Mom, and I left France with our friends from Fort Worth. We took a train to Lucerne, Switzerland and hung out for a few days. There were swans on the lake, and we went on a paddleboat and had to endure Sarah talking about how much fun she had had with her friends in France. She spoke of this at the lake, restaurants, a jewelry store, and in the hotel room.

Bringing the same subject up incessantly in the same 24-hour period was a favorite habit of Sarah's at the time. She once took a class on Joan of Arc in college and thereafter associated every attempt we made at conversation to something about Joan of Arc.

Me: *So, my birthday's coming up.*

Sarah: *That's right, Rachel! How old are you turning?*

Me: *I'll be 18.*

Sarah: *Did you know that Joan of Arc was only 19 years old when she died?*

Or the time Dad was getting ready for a cookout in the backyard.

Sarah: *Oh, you're starting a fire? That's nice. Did you know that Joan of Arc was burned alive?*

She went on and on all evening about it. We all got so tired of it that at the end of the cookout our cousin Andrew finally said, "Oh, she was? Well, you're about to see what it feels like."

But I digress.

From Switzerland we took a train across the Alps to Italy. It was so hot on the train—the air conditioner went out halfway through the trip—that the back of my knees began to sweat. But there was a dining cart where I got a big lunch, which I thoroughly enjoyed—that is, until the train started tilting on its way through the mountains and everything in my stomach tilted with it.

We visited Venice, which they call the City on Stilts because it's built in a lagoon, but really it should be called the City on Stairs, since every five yards there's a stairway you have to haul your suitcase over. We somehow arrived at the hotel before dusk and then went to eat.

I wish I had something romantic to say, like there was a boy I had left behind in France who followed me to Italy and surprised me by helping me pull my suitcase up the stairs. But there wasn't. Nothing happened at all, except I did eat seafood pasta and stayed awake all night throwing it up.

GGG's Lessons for Surviving Travel

❀ Always check if peanut butter is considered contraband in your country of destination.

❀ Remember to record your sister constantly bringing up the same subject so you can show it to her when she says she doesn't do that.

❀ Always drink Italian lemon soda after vomiting.

CHAPTER 12

SURF AND SPANISH

Another thing Mom thought would look good on our college resumes was knowing a foreign language, other than English (!), so we focused on learning Spanish during our homeschool years. She taught us Spanish grammar all through elementary and middle school, but when we reached high school, she thought it was time for us to actually learn to speak it. And because she must have had short-term memory loss about our experience in France, she thought it would be good to take the whole family to Costa Rica during the summer. It was going to be a two-week trip with our friends the Brantleys (remember, from GAPP fame?), who also wanted their kids to study Spanish. Apparently, they were as crazy as we were.

So we all dutifully packed our suitcases—no peanut butter jars this time—for our Costa Rican "vacation." I put "vacation" in quotation marks because we went to a tropical Central American country in the middle of summer—the hottest and most humid time of year!—and we still had to attend school there to study Spanish. We stayed in a town called Tamarindo, which is big on surfing...so much so that our class schedule changed according to the tides. Cowabunga, dude.

We took surfing lessons from a blond Costa Rican guy named Junior. Cool, right? Well, Sarah didn't think his name should be Junior—I suppose it wasn't stereotypically Latino enough for her—so she decided to call him Pedro. Sarah often gives new names to people, especially when the one they have doesn't fit the image she has of them in her head. We all follow her in this endeavor, young and old alike, to the point that we forget the people's actual names. When Mrs. Brantley absent-mindedly said, "Thanks, Pedro," after our last surfing lesson, and he looked around, confused, it was just one part of a greater lesson about Sarah—no one can spend any time with her and stay the same person; you have to assume a new identity to conform with her notion of who you are meant to be.

The language school was comprised mostly of open classrooms to let the air blow in, except there was no air, just humid moisture thick enough to turn your hair into a frizzy mop. Sarah, Meg (the Brantley daughter my age) and I were in a class with a mid-20s teacher named Gilberto. Gilberto was easygoing, had a button of Che Guevara on his bookbag and had never heard of the band Green Day. How could one function properly in society without knowledge of Green Day?! But somehow he managed.

The other student was a mid-20s American named Blaine. I felt bad for him. I imagined he probably came to Costa Rica in the hopes of "learning Spanish" with a group of cute college girls and having some surfing fun and romance. Instead, he was stuck with three annoying pre-teen girls.

The room was like a large balcony with a grass-woven roof. We all sat at a big wooden table with matching wooden chairs. We went around the room and introduced ourselves in Spanish, and Blaine, wearing a baseball cap and regretful expression, said, *Hola, me llamo Blaine...*

"*Blame?*" Gilberto asked, confused.

"No, *Blaine.*"

"Ah, *flame*, like a fire."

"No, *Blaine.*"

Apparently the name Blaine doesn't exist in Spanish, and we were all having way too much fun with Gilberto messing up Blaine's name. The next day of class Gilberto called him John Wayne (Blaine/Wayne, get it?).

On the third day, in order to avoid another 20 minutes of Gilberto trying to figure out Blaine's name, Sarah took matters into her own hands and decided we would all begin calling him James.

As Blaine walked into the classroom, he said, *Hola, buenos días.*

Sarah responded, *Hola, James, qué tal?*

He looked bewildered as we all laughed devilishly. And that's the last time anybody called him Blaine. From then on we all referred to him as "James," to the point that when we were all going out for dinner after class, Mr. Brantley asked, "Did you ask James if he would like to join us?"

Poor guy—how we liked to pick on him. One time during class, we pretended to eat his cake. There was a little lunch area where all the students went during break that sold pieces of cake and sandwiches. James—I mean, Blaine—bought a piece of cake and put it on the table warning us, "Do *not* eat this!" When he went off somewhere, maybe to make a call or go to the bathroom, we took the piece of cake, hid it under the table, and left a few crumbs on his plate. When he returned, he did not react well to the practical joke, so we gave him his cake back pretty quickly.

James/Blaine got a respite the second week when a girl named Mandy joined the class. She was around his age and wore shorts and a little scarf in her hair and had white nail polish she picked off during class. That was one of the no-no's I'd learned about in my week of etiquette class that I actually agreed with. I thought we all got along great, but I guess we rubbed her the wrong way because during a class break one day she said to us, "Could you guys not talk in English during class, cause I'm really trying to get this."

We looked at her for a second and I guffawed, thinking she was joking. Note: I'm usually the one who responds inappropriately in sensitive situations, like the time our fifth grade history teacher at GAPP yelled at us for being too loud and I pulled my hair by my face and said, "Do I look like George Washington?"

But Mandy wasn't joking. The truth was, we never talked amongst ourselves in English during class, but she was probably looking for a way to express her profound irritation for our constant giggling and general giddiness. We all glanced at James to see if he was on our side, but he had assumed the typical "keep me out of this" expression men have when girls fight.

Costa Rica for the most part was a blast, but towards the end of the second week, our conversations began to lag. When you're exclusively with the same group of people for a long time, you eventually run out of topics because they're with you everywhere you go, so there's no new news. Hannah (the other Brantley daughter) and Sarah would begin to make up stories about the people in the restaurants just so we would have stuff to talk about. Thankfully, one evening a mariachi band decided to surround our table for an entire song and play as loudly as possible next to my right ear while everybody in the restaurant stared at us. I'd seen this guy at the bar request the song, and I'm pretty sure he purposefully sent the band to our table, for which I was going to go beat him up, but we were in Costa Rica and I wasn't familiar with their penal system—so I decided against it. At least the band gave us something to talk about. That was the only bad part of Costa Rica. Well, that and the fact that I was on the top bunk in the bedroom and the ladder only went halfway to the floor, so I literally had to jump out of bed every morning.

GGG's LESSONS FOR SURVIVING SPANISH CLASSES IN COSTA RICA

❀ Always pre-screen your Spanish classes for the prissy American girl.

❀ Make sure you have a completely closed classroom in a tropical Central American country if you don't want an iguana coming in and almost falling on your head.

❀ Older sisters can be very influential. My name would be Regina if I had let Sarah get her way.

CHAPTER 13

SPANISH—TAKE TWO!

Although the Costa Rica trip was successful, Mom did not think we'd become sufficiently fluent during our time there, so she chose Mexico for our next learning venue. The following summer, we rented a house in a nice little coastal town called Playa del Carmen on the Yucatan Peninsula about 40 miles south of Cancun, where there was a Spanish language school. She thought a month would be a good amount of time to firm up our Spanish skills.

The house was really cute, and there were beaches and palm trees, and breezes and manatees. Actually, there weren't any manatees, I just wanted to make it rhyme. But there were iguanas.

The trouble with visiting a foreign country when you have strict parents who don't let you spend the night at other people's houses or listen to Justin Timberlake is that you get all your notions about new places from the movies they *do* let you watch. So when we checked into our house by the beach, I assumed it was going to be like *From Justin to Kelly* or some other spring break movie, combined with an adventure flick like *Holiday in the Sun*, where you get lost and solve conspiracy mysteries and somehow a cute Mexican guy fits in the mix.

Not.

Every time I wanted to go outside of the house, I had to tag along with Sarah or Dad or Mom. Since you couldn't go out with either of my parents (all Mom wanted to do was read on the beach and Dad liked to speak English loudly with a Mexican accent—his version of speaking Spanish), I went out with Sarah, but not without the mandatory stranger/danger talk from Mom.

"Don't talk to strangers or look at strangers or go anywhere with strangers and if any stranger tries to talk to you or get you to go anywhere or do anything, first you scream, then you get Rachel to kick them, and then you call me."

It was even worse when we wanted to go out at night. "Do you know what happens to young girls when they go out in Mexico alone at night?" Mom asked. "They get kidnapped and people kill them and sell their organs! DO you want people to kidnap you and sell your organs?!?!"

"I don't know. What's the going rate?"

I kept that one to myself.

These warnings reminded me of the times at home when we were old enough and Mom would leave me and Sarah alone in the car for a few seconds to run into the convenience store to grab something.

Before she took off, she would say, "Lock the door and don't open it for anyone—not even for Mr. Patterson."

Now, Mr. Patterson was a family friend and the nicest, most trustworthy guy you will ever know, and she used him as an extreme example to drive home the point that we weren't allowed to open the door for *anyone at all.*

Well, one day we were in front of the grocery store and Mom had run in to get some milk. Sarah and I were listening to a Hilary Duff CD, when who of all people happened to appear in the parking lot? You guessed it—Mr. Patterson!

"Rachel, Sarah! Hi!"

We had to talk to him through the closed window. "Oh, this is awkward. Sorry, Mr. Patterson, but we're under specific orders not to open the door for you."

So it was not surprising that Mom would not let us walk but instead drove us to the Spanish school herself, which was only 10 minutes from the house.

The first day there the administrator put all the new students in a room to give us an overview of what lay ahead. All of the classes would be conducted in Spanish, and we were forbidden to speak any English. I was going to inform her that I don't talk anyway—I just glare—but I thought I would save that bit of information for another day. Normally, people would be nervous about making a good first impression on the first day of class. Not me, though. I just assume that nobody is going to like me and go from there.

After the orientation, we went to meet our teacher, whose name was Fernando. We sat around a rectangular table, with Fernando at the head near the chalkboard. There were a bunch of international students in class with us, between the ages of 24 and 35. There was a Swiss French girl, a Dutch guy named Sven, a Swiss German, an American, and two German girls who were really loud and annoying and got kicked out of class by Fernando, so I don't think they count.

There was a nightclub in the area called "The Blue Parrot" that all the students, but not us, would go to on the weekends and on Wednesdays (because that was 'ladies night'). Except for Sven—he would go pretty much every night. Most mornings he wouldn't come to the first session because he was not fit for class—if you know what I mean—but we always saved his seat just in case and Fernando would say that he was with us "in spirit" (not realizing he'd made a joke).

It seemed poor Sven was always hungover when he showed up for class and one day he asked me, "You think I just party all the time, don't you?"

"Noooo…Maybe. Actually, yes."

Fernando was one of the funniest teachers I have ever had. He taught us lots of important things, like how to understand Mexican history and how to spot if someone was German by noting they're wearing knee socks with sandals.

One class day we were all talking about how we said "ouch" in our different languages. Everybody contributed in their respective languages, but Sven didn't really remember how to say "ouch" in Dutch, so Fernando lifted his book over Sven's head and smacked him with it, saying, "We are going to learn a little bit of Dutch today."

"Au!" Sven exclaimed—and there it was.

During the weekends, we actually were allowed to have fun. There was a stand where you could go sign up for snorkeling and parasailing. One Friday, Mom, Sarah and I went to sign up for parasailing for the next day. Eduardo, the guy who ran the stand, thought my mom was cute and started hitting on her like nobody's business. He said her eyes were "full of beautiful color" (they're brown) and kept talking to her the whole time she was filling out the forms. Before we left he made sure to tell her, "I will dream *with* you tonight." Instead of, "I will dream *of* you tonight." I know he said it that way because his English wasn't perfect, but it was still creepy.

Needless to say, Mom didn't want to go parasailing the next day in order to avoid Eduardo. So my dad went with us instead and she stayed at the house with the boys.

When we got to the stand, Eduardo was there, waiting to take us to the dock.

"Is your mom not here?" he asked. We could see disappointment in his eyes.

"Uh, no, she's not here," Sarah said.

I pushed Dad forward. "But this is my dad, her *husband*, the father of her *four* children. *Cuatro*!"

"So she's not coming?"

Seriously, dude?

"No. She's not coming."

He looked so sad that Sarah couldn't help but add a "sorry," but then Dad elbowed her.

"What? I feel bad for the guy. Look how sad he is!"

"Are you for real, Sarah? Do *not* apologize!"

Thankfully, Eduardo didn't come parasailing with us, but he so would have if Mom had been there.

Parasailing was cool, but I kept wishing that I had brought Michael's Nerf gun with me so I could shoot at all the little people below me while I was flying.

We had a lot of fun in Playa del Carmen. Leaving was hard because the food was awesome, the weather was great, and there was cable at the rental house, something not allowed in our home in Texas. We never even had basic cable. I grew up with just five basic channels, although I did have unlimited access to *Teenage Mutant Ninja Turtles*, which is the only show you really need when you're a pre-teen.

The day we packed, there was a guy on the beach that I had spotted a couple of days before. He waved goodbye to us as we got in the car, so I guess I did get a little bit of a spring break movie romance after all. Hah!

Our Spanish improved considerably but nobody cares about that when an imaginary romance is at hand.

GGG's Lessons for Surviving Traveling to Mexico

✿ Always make sure your organs are insured.

✿ Always keep your eyes open for a possible romance.

✿ Pretend you don't hear your mother when she says, "You never need to take either of these precautions."

CHAPTER 14

ME + MATH = ZERO

By the time I was a sophomore in high school, Mom was looking ahead to the SATs. Knowing that math was a major portion of the test, and realizing that her math capabilities didn't exceed the second half of geometry, she hired tutors to teach me advanced algebra and trigonometry. One was a guy in his late 20s—I'll call him Igor (fake name)—who came to our house every Thursday to improve my Algebra II skills. Things started out well enough; we actually got along and I was pretty receptive, but the minute I realized he got his nails manicured, I was done.

We live in the country and so our house sits on some acreage. The entrance gate is situated several yards before you get to the house, and people have to ring the bell and we push a button from the house to let them in. Every Thursday, I'd run throughout the house turning down all the intercoms so that Mom wouldn't hear the bell. But she caught me doing that one time and said that if I missed a lesson, I had to make up for it twice. So I decided the better plan would be to torment Igor until he quit, like all my other teachers. I argued with him about politics, theology and philosophy. One time I actually called him "crazy" (which, of course, he wasn't, but I was desperate). To his credit, he stuck it out to the bitter end and didn't make any excuses, such as having to leave to go help the African natives, like my former piano teacher. In my defense, teaching me actually comes with a lot of benefits. Apparently, those who stick with me for a whole teaching cycle automatically qualify to become Navy Seals.

I ended up getting an A in Algebra II, all due to my hard work and blood, sweat and tears! Well, *his* sweat and tears, mostly, but I made a small contribution.

During that same year, I got to learn how to drive. You might not think that there's such a thing as homeschool driver's ed—but there is. And guess who had to learn driving on homeschooling driver's ed?

Yes, she did.

I did all the stuff about traffic rules and regulations on the computer, and my dad took me on practice drives (because my mom didn't let me change lanes when I drove with her if there was another car on the road—anywhere within five miles— kidding!) I actually got my driver's license the first time I took my test, which was pretty cool. Driver's ed was probably the only category in life where I outdid Sarah. She didn't really study for the test portion of driver's ed and had to retake it. I made sure to revel in that for a few days and mention it every time she tried to tell me how to drive the car.

The first time I drove without Sarah or my parents in the car was when my cousin Katie came for a visit. We were headed to the movies

10 minutes away from our house and the whole time I chanted, "My parents are going to kill me. My parents are going to kill me."

Katie asked, "Why would they kill you? They know you're driving."

"Yes, but something bad is going to happen. It always does. And then they're going to kill me."

Thankfully, nothing bad happened, for once, but when Katie and I got home that evening, there was an extra car in the driveway.

"Whoa, whose car is that?" I asked Katie rhetorically. We almost never had visitors at night.

"I don't know," she answered absentmindly. She didn't seem interested, and I'm sure she didn't even know what I asked since she was typing on her iPhone. I had already noticed that she got enough text messages to single-handedly keep Verizon in business for an entire year.

But I was intrigued. What was it with the mystery car? Who was here? Why didn't Mom tell me someone was coming? Then it hit me. Mom didn't tell me when someone was coming over if she knew I didn't like that person. If I knew ahead of time, I'd refuse to come home until I was sure that person had left. I had been trapped! But by whom?

I didn't realize that I sat immobile, frozen in the driver's seat of the car, until Katie asked, "Aren't we going inside?"

I reluctantly got out of the car and headed toward the house. As we entered the foyer, I gingerly closed the door so as to not draw attention to myself and started to tiptoe toward the stairs. Katie, however, looked like she was headed to the living room.

"SssshhHH! Katie, don't go in there!"

"Why not? Everyone's in that room."

"Exactly!"

We were halfway on our way to freedom when a voice erupted from within the house. "Where do you want me to put the calculus books?"

Threat Level 4! Panic mode!! It was Igor, my manicured math tutor!!!

Katie asked naively, "Shouldn't we go in there?"

She has so much to learn.

I was trying to employ the Jurassic Park T-Rex strategy: If I don't move, they can't see me. But it didn't work this time. Probably because Katie walked into the living room and introduced herself. I, of course, needed no introduction. Why was he here? I had been doing okay with my cousin, Andrew, tutoring me. He had been teaching me trigonometry while Igor took a break, probably to admit himself into an emotional rehab facility. But recently Mom had threatened to hire him again, just to spite me, I suppose. Well, it was no threat. He was back and ready to tutor me again. Like I said, Navy Seals.

I had to study calculus with him for the rest of the year. I maintained a good two feet between us during lessons and employed my signature expressionless-bored face as often as possible. All to no avail. He didn't quit until the school year was over.

GGG's Lessons for Surviving Your Math Teacher

✿ It's not always necessary to go inside. What do you think people did before they invented houses?

✿ Like Hilary Duff said, "If you can't do the math, then get out of the equation."

✿ Velociraptors can see your every move.

CHAPTER 15

SCIENCE IS AS EASY AS PIE

Science always presented me with an interesting conundrum. To be honest, it just isn't my strong suit. I don't know if all writers feel that way or if it's just me, but I don't really care to understand how the universe and its components work. I wake up—the sun is out. I go to bed—the sun has set. It works—and that's good enough for me.

If I have to learn something about how the world works, I personally prefer the mythological views of science and strongly advocate the reinstatement of its teachings into our schools. Why does spring change into winter? Because that is when Hades takes Demeter's daughter Persephone back to the underworld and Demeter mourns until he returns her. Why do earthquakes and tidal waves and sea storms occur? Because Poseidon is really short tempered, especially when certain individuals attack his Cyclops son and poke his eye out; then he wreaks havoc with his triton! This is how it should be taught, none of this "tectonic plates" and "gravitational pull of the moon" nonsense they torture us with today.

But Mom refused to leave it at Demeter and Persephone, and during our elementary and junior high years, she taught us science at home. I remember when I was in seventh grade, Mom thought she would have us do a little "hands on" learning when we got to the biology section of our book. So, she ordered a dried frog on the Internet and invited my friend Carley over to participate in its dissection with me. Apparently, there is nothing you can't order online, including wax tablets, microscopes and formaldehyde.

One fine Saturday afternoon the frog arrived courtesy of UPS, and we had a biology lab experience. Carley and I basically cut the frog into pieces and learned nothing.

I brought it inside the house and showed Sarah, and she said something like, "Oh! How disgusting!" and shoved me outside, locking the door.

I tried, "Okay, Sarah, I threw it away…"

"I don't believe you. You are a lying, little frog-dissecting brat. I'm not letting you back inside the house until you get rid of it!"

I tried to feed it to our dog, but she didn't seem to want it (I guess she didn't know it was an *educational lunch*), so I took it to the pond near our house and set its various parts free in its original habitat.

That was the last time Mom let me take science into my own hands.

Once we got to high school, Mom wanted us to take some courses beyond her expertise, taught by "official" educational institutions, because she wanted us to learn the stuff and also because she figured an official school class would add some validity to the college application. She didn't think it looked right if every class we took was taught by her—it would somehow make having straight A's look suspect. So, we took some online classes and enrolled once again in another MWF school for science and a couple of other courses.

By this point I had kind of forgotten what "real" school was like, but I had watched most of *Grease* at least 15 times, which gave me a clue as to what went on there. I said *most of Grease* because Mom always made us fast-forward through the parts she deemed inappropriate for impressionable young minds. Can you imagine?

Anyway, I had this weird notion that school would be a bit like the movie, so I thought, "This is gonna be awesome!" But there were no drag races, tattoos, or synchronized dancing. I should have left my leather pants at home that first day, too, but nobody warned me.

The school had a small cafeteria where all they sold was basically junk food—my favorite! One day during lunch, I was thoughtfully chewing a Three Musketeers bar and looked at the wrapper, which had printed on it, "25% LESS FAT," in yellow letters. That got me thinking: 25% less fat than what? Than something with 25% more fat? Or 25% less fat than what it used to have, in which case I would like to return this candy bar. They do that with toothpaste, too. "30% more effective!" More effective than what? I guess it's about truth in advertising, but what is the point of truth if it makes no sense?

I have little memory of most of the science courses I took at the MWF school, since I mostly tune out what I don't like, but we did have a unique physics teacher in 11th grade. I'll call him Mr. Poindexter. The first day of class he bounded into the room sporting thick white hair and a tie decorated with small rhinos, then he handed each one of the students a five dollar bill. "I like to get my students' attention before I start teaching," he explained, "and the best way to get people's attention is with money! So here you go!"

Everybody sat up straighter and put the bill up to the light to see if it was fake. Free money! The best way to start class!

Mr. Poindexter also decided he didn't like the physics texts the school provided, so he gave us all college-level books that he had bought and paid for himself, because "the ones the school gave you are too easy and these don't have questions about apple pie."

That quickly became an inside joke among us; any easy question was an "apple pie" question. There were very few of those, however, because it was a college physics textbook, so we couldn't use the joke as often as we would have liked.

Mr. Poindexter was fun but eccentric—much like you would expect from a physics teacher, with his head in the clouds. He would often forget what he was saying or doing. Like one day during class he said, "You all want to hear a joke?" We nodded eagerly—anything to get off the subject. Encouraged, he started, "A giraffe walked into a bar and left a tip on the barstool…no wait, he did something else first… he said to the bartender 'I'm not a lion, I'm a giraffe…' Ah, I forget. Anyway, we're not here to make jokes, we're here to learn science."

During my senior year, I took an anatomy course at the MWF school. On the first day of class, the teacher gave us the following speech: "You all here are adults and we will treat you as adults." I almost raised my hand to tell her that I was still a juvenile—she could check with my mom for confirmation—but I decided against it for the time being. Then she explained that she used the acronym SLANT for the behavior she expected of us.

S—Sit up

L—Look at the teacher

A—Always raise your hand

N—Nod if you are paying attention

T—Track the teacher's eyes

Oh, yeah, you are *so* treating us like adults.

I almost asked when nap time was scheduled but feared the wrath of Khan, I mean Mom. To my surprise, I actually ended up liking the teacher—she was a nurse and really knew her stuff, and by some miracle she liked me as well. Go figure.

GGG's Lessons for Surviving Science

✿ Only a few people in the world need to understand science, and they can explain it to the rest of us condescendingly when necessary.

✿ Don't get out of bed for physics for less than $5 a day.

✿ Apple pie questions are 30% less effective.

CHAPTER 16

LET'S PARTY!

My mom is a firm believer in self-improvement. A year earlier, she had made me read *How to Win Friends and Influence People*. Apparently my state at that time was *How to Scare Friends and Traumatize People* (Igor and Bob both could have written little back cover testimonials).

Despite reading the book, I hadn't won many friends. Whenever I would try to integrate into a social group at MWF school, I experienced an interesting dilemma. I was never really a *part* of a group; I was sort of the general advisor. I was the one they asked questions of, sat next to in order to get answers about homework, and imparted private information to (since they couldn't tell their actual friends, who treated secrets like that kid from *Free Willy* treated the whale. They let them go free, is what I'm saying). I knew I was being used, and to console myself I pretended I was The Grand Vizier—like the guy in *Aladdin*—and smugly pictured myself wearing a purple robe and turban.

One day, one of the kids in class was having a party and, for a change, I got invited. I was a bit panicked, so I decided to review *How to Win Friends*...a bit. I didn't actually find anything that would be useful to me that evening—I just reread the part where the guy tells the story of when he was nice to an old lady and she gave him a car. I didn't exactly know how that would help me out with my friends at the party.

I wanted to look nice, so I painted my nails. I put on some OPI nail polish, which I use partly because it's good nail polish and partly because of the names they have for their colors: "Austin-tatious Turquoise," "Lucerne-tainly Look Marvelous," "St. Petersburgundy." Who comes up with these names? How can I get that job? Seriously— I could *so* do that job!

Anyway, Mom walked in as I was painting my nails and said, "Oh, this nail polish looks good! What color is it?"

"You're Such a Kabuki Queen."

"*Excuse me?!*"

"Pink."

Sarah was in college by then, but was visiting for the weekend. I asked her to help me pick out clothes because I have a habit of being overdressed, which further exaggerates the problem of being stranger than everybody else.

As I was putting on a skirt, she said, "Please try to act interesting tonight."

"What are you insinuating? That I'm *boring?*"

"Sometimes you slouch and talk like a gorilla."

"A gorilla?! Fine! You just wait, I will be loquacious to a fault."

"*Loquacious?* Are you serious?"

As I thought about what she said, I figured it might help if she went with me to the party. Sarah loves parties, so I didn't have to beg all that hard. She went to her room and came back out in a dress that clasped around the neck and came down in folds and layers.

"How do I look?"

"Like a curtain."

"Is that good or bad?"

"That depends—do you like curtains?"

She glared at me and went to get the car keys.

We arrived at my friend's house. There were a lot of people milling around the front yard. We entered the house, which was spacious with wooden floors. People lounged around the living room, talking and occasionally erupting in laughter. I recognized most people there from my MWF classes. Even though we arrived a bit late, I was eager to try to fit in. I immediately whipped out my socializing skills.

Me: *Hey, homies. What's up in the hizzah?*

Friends: *...Uh... nothing much...*

Me: *Yo' threads be fly, diggity dawg.*

Friends: *What?*

Sarah (pulling me away): *She likes to mix her energy drinks.*

Me: *Keep it real!!!*

Sarah saw somebody she knew and abandoned me. I quietly merged with a group of girls talking by the soda bar. I listened for a few seconds to find out they were talking about a show I wasn't allowed to watch, and as I'd never seen an episode, I turned to find some snacks—only to run into Jason Kemp.

Who was Jason Kemp? Well, I'll tell you: He was the only person I knew who I hadn't scared or intimidated. Why? Because every time I was around him, I always switched the first letters of my words around because, for some reason, he made me nervous. Was it because he was good-looking? Maybe. Or because he was smart? Perhaps. But I didn't have time to fully analyze it at the time before he spoke.

"Hey, Rachel! What's up?! Are you here alone?"

"No, Sarah's here with me."

I pointed to the right where Sarah was not standing, but I didn't know where she was and I felt like I should make some kind of a gesture.

"Cool, so how've you been?"

"Fine, just school and beading rooks."

He didn't miss a beat. "Beading rooks? What rooks have you been beading?"

Mom had recently had us reading *Quo Vadis*. But I decided that my very existence was strange enough and I didn't need to tell him I was reading that book. I was gonna think of something else.

"*Quo Vadis.*"

Danggit!

"What?"

"Um, I mean *Eragon*."

Back home that night, I looked up educational opportunities in Tibet. Even that may not be far enough away to overcome my awkwardness with Jason Kemp and the entire institution of MWF high school.

GGG's Lessons for Surviving Parties

✿ **Don't talk unless necessary.**

✿ **Watch some TV, for goodness' sake, to learn teenage vernacular.**

✿ **Stay away from Jason Kemp.**

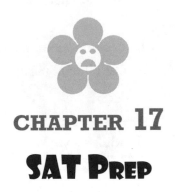

CHAPTER 17

SAT PREP

By now we were getting to the point in my high school career where I had to start preparing for the SAT. The first thing Mom made me study for was the essay. Although I like to write, I can't really write *SAT* essays. They ask you tricky questions and my first tendency is to say what my brain immediately thinks. And you all know that cannot be anything good. Here's an example:

> *Is conscience a more powerful motivator than money, fame or power?*

My answer was:

> *Conscience is only something for the weak who do not have enough courage to stand up for what is rightfully theirs. Selfishness is for the strong. "Being kind" and "putting others first" is for wusses. Fame lasts forever and so does money. Power is what everyone wants and everyone will envy you if you have it!* **Muahahaha!**

Of course I don't believe any of that but inexplicably that's what my brain said at first, and that's what I wrote on the practice exams. Well, minus the evil laugh. But my mom looked online for corrective lunatic camps anyway, and I was sent upstairs to read 1 Corinthians 13 for the millionth time: "If I speak in the tongues of men or of angels, but do not have love, I am only a resounding gong or a clanging cymbal." Resounding gong—that sounds about right.

So, on the following practice essays, I started out pretty well but began to go downhill toward the end. Here's another example:

> *Do changes that make our lives easier not necessarily make them better?*

My answer was:

> *It is true that advances in science and medicine have eliminated most of life's uncertainties, but changes in the field of technology do not necessarily have the same effect. In today's society, technology has become a substitute for aspects of life that were intended to be fuller. Our reliance on technology has degraded the way we socialize and the proper way to interact with our peers.*

(Pretty good so far, right?)

But then I went "off the reservation" and continued:

> *Instead of interacting with our fellow man, we interact on Facebook. People only post stories of doing something they think will make you jealous. Their ‹status updates› are never "Hey, I am such a loser." They're usually more like, "I just had dinner with Brad Pitt!!!" We get false advertising because the only pictures we see are those that make people look skinny, when actually they are BIG FAT COWS! I'm right. You're wrong. The end.*

So this preparation stuff was gonna take a little longer than I initially anticipated. And it was torture. When I wasn't at MWF school or homeschooling with Mom, I had to be studying for the SAT. If I had a single free moment, Mom would make me feel guilty if I wasn't doing a practice exam. One Friday night I woke up at 3 a.m., unable to sleep. Worried that she somehow would know that I hadn't used my sleepless hours "wisely," I grabbed the SAT prep book and turned to the math section.

Here are some of the problems I read:

> **Question 1:** *Salwa has a set of knives that costs 25 dollars. If Salwa earns 40 dollars a day and gives ⅓ of this away, how long will she have to save up until she can buy a new set of similar knives?*

I thought the more important question is why the heck Salwa needed so many knives. What exactly *were* you planning, Salwa??

> **Question 2:** *Kai is at a party in a room of 200 people who are divided into 16 rows. If people with 2 vowels in their names are the 5th in the row starting from the back, where is Kai?*

My answer was that he must be off to do something more interesting. That sounded like the lamest party ever. But that wasn't an option among the possible answers.

> **Question 3:** *Ahiambo and Hiroshi leave a house at the same time. If Ahiambo walks due north at 30 miles per hour and Hiroshi walks due east at 40 miles per hour, what will be the distance between them at the end of 3 hours?*

I began to notice a pattern with these questions. They kept using a bunch of foreign names like "Ming" or "Saleem" or "Baldroubaldour." I guess they're trying to compensate for the cruel and unusual punishment by being politically correct, which just made it even more complicated because I spent an extra half minute trying to pronounce all the names in my head.

I took a break from studying and thought about why I hated the topic of college so much, and I realized one of the reasons was that the idea of college interviews made me nervous. I was scared that I would forget my interests and ambitions and say that my favorite movie was *Titanic* or something equally inane.

The reason for my fear may have been because of Sarah's college interviews. When Sarah went in to meet with somebody at one of her college interviews, Mom and I drove her. After it was over, and on the way back in the car, my mom said, "How was your first college interview?"

At first Sarah didn't answer, but Mom insisted, "What kind of questions did they ask?"

"Oh, you know, what are your ambitions? If you could meet one person in the world who would it be?"

I interjected, "Who did you say?"

No reply.

"Sarah, answer your sister."

Silence.

"Cleopatra."

Mom and I both snorted. "Cleopatra?!?! Why did you say *Cleopatra?*"

"I don't know," Sarah said, aggravated. "The girl before me said Marie Antoinette, and I didn't know who to say, so I said Cleopatra."

The second interview was farther way, so I didn't go along for the ride. But soon after Sarah returned home, I poked my head in her room.

"So," I asked, "how was the interview?"

"Fine."

"Did you mention Cleopatra again?"

"I don't wanna talk about it."

"You did?!?!"

"Go away!" She slammed the door.

She did!!!

Artists!

GGG's Lessons for Surviving SATs and College Interviews

✿ Make sure to leave Mr. Hyde at home and take Dr. Jekyll to the SAT.

✿ Try to get out of taking the SAT by saying there are not enough ethnicities represented in the questions.

✿ During college interviews, if you think it's good to mention the Queen of the Nile, then you're the Queen of De-Nial.

CHAPTER 18

TEST DAY TORTURE

After months of studying, it was time to take the SAT. The test was held at a ridiculous hour. The College Board apparently loves to find ways to make you get up way earlier in the morning than is good for anyone and make you do something you don't want to do for hours. You won't fully understand what I'm saying until you have to wake up at 6 a.m. on a Saturday and drive to the nearest local high school to fill in thousands of bubbles for five hours—bubbles that will ultimately determine your future.

So I found myself on the Saturday in question sitting on a bench outside of Burleson High School, yawning and feeling like I needed toothpicks for my eyelids, waiting for the administrators to let us in. I may be grumpy in my usual walk of life, but that morning I was downright mean.

I was surprised to see my cousin Jeremy approaching from a distance. He waved and walked up to me. "Hey, Rach! I didn't know you were gonna be here. You here to take the SAT?"

"No, *Jeremy,* I just like waking up Saturday mornings at 6 a.m. to come hang out at Burleson High School with a calculator and #2 pencil."

He wasn't expecting that and slowly backed away with a nervous laugh. That was mean, even for me, but I'm taking the opportunity to blame all my inappropriate behavior on the SAT because normally I am so calm and serene.

As I looked around at the other students waiting, I realized that taking the SAT is one of the few times when you can wear whatever you want and no one cares or judges you. Pajama pants and an AC/DC t-shirt? Sweet. Gladiator sandals and a puffy jacket? Right on. I saw people with three different headbands, high-rise short shorts, sparkly boots and Michael Jackson-padded jackets. And guess what? *No one* even cared. When you're all in the same sinking ship, it doesn't matter what anybody is wearing—you're all going to drown anyway. That's why I decided to pull a Lady Godiva and not wear anything. *Kidding!* I wore sweatpants, sandals and a shirt with the words "Break it Down, Shake it Down" that I had gotten three years earlier. Nothing at all probably would have been better.

After the doors opened, we all shuffled in line half asleep until the moment we sat down at the assigned desks. Everybody knows the rules of how to take standardized tests, but the people administering the test have to read them out loud to you anyway.

> *Turn off any cellular devices or any wristwatches that make noises to indicate the passing of an hour. If at any time during examination your phone goes off, your test will be completely nullified. If you must leave at any time during examination, your scores will be completely nullified. If you are found to be in any way cheating during the examination, your scores will be completely nullified.*

Something about the word "nullified" made the testing situation a far more stressful experience than it needed to be. I don't know why but it gave me visions of having to live with my parents the rest of my life.

They directed us to the back of the testing sheet where there was a statement that read something like,

> *I promise not to copy any questions or reveal the content of this test to anyone outside the testing room in conversation, email, or by phone because we really know that when you're finally finished with this, all you're going to want to do is talk about it.*

Then we had to rewrite the statement in cursive and sign it. Why in cursive, I don't know. I learned cursive in the third grade and I had never had the occasion to use it until this point. Mom always told me I'd need it later on in life, but I didn't know it would be for *this*.

The essay question sounded like one of Sarah's college interview questions.

> *Do you think that our fears make us more cautious or cause a debilitating mentality?*

I was going to write how when I travel I always get paranoid that I forgot my retainer at home and will have to get braces again, but I didn't think that would be "serious" enough for the College Board, so I wrote something about "Avatar: The Last Airbender," the animated TV show, when Aang's fear of burning someone again kept him from mastering his firebending skills. Now that I think back on it, the retainer thing might have been better.

Five wrist-cramping hours later, we were done.

I was on my way home when Mom texted me with the following message: *Can you pick up some parsley for me?*

Ugh! Who uses decorative vegetation anyway? But I did as she asked and trudged through the side door of the house.

The torture that is my life continued when I walked into the kitchen. My mom and my aunts were cooking for a dinner party, and Michael and John David were attacking everybody with inflatable swords.

My uncle was there, too, not actually helping but providing a running commentary, "The food needs more garlic and onion."

The rice, the chicken, the beef, the ice cream—it all needed more garlic and onion—and it was obvious my mom was getting tired of it.

She piped up. "Say, why don't you go jogging with Nabil? He's about to go. You might enjoy it."

"No, I don't want to go. Jogging makes me tired."

I thought to myself, "Really, slim?"

My dad, who had been listening to my uncle's culinary advice from the living room, interjected, "Don't worry, I'll just put a necklace of garlic and onion around my neck and you can run after me."

That got my uncle out of the kitchen.

I really needed to veg out after five hours of the SAT and my family in the kitchen, so I called my cousin Andrew to see if he would go to the movies with me. He mercifully said yes, and I made him go see the movie *Post Grad*. Not only was it too close for comfort—this girl played by Alexis Bledel graduates from college but can't find a job, so she moves back in with her crazy family and nearly loses her sanity—but it was just plain awful. I'm telling you about it now to spare you the mistake of renting it online. I don't have many talents, but I do have this innate ability of picking the most dreadful movies and making other people watch them with me. But it is not my fault;

the trailers make them look good! I may have a career in focus groups that test which morons to market these movies to.

Anyway, we were sitting at the front of the theater, and as the movie was starting, a girl at the very back started talking very loudly on her cell phone.

With my new post-etiquette camp mentality, I couldn't help but ask myself how I could implement what I had learned in daily situations. So, I was racking my brain about what would be proper decorum—as the girl in the back continued her rudeness.

"What?! No! I'm at the movies! I can't hear you! Speak louder!"

It's one of those situations that makes you capable of doing something that might land you in prison. I think you know what I mean. This chick was choosing to ignore all of the universal be-quiet signs, including glares, stares, and tsks, and kept on yammering really loudly.

While I kept dithering, trying to formulate an etiquette-appropriate response, Andrew suddenly stood up, turned around and yelled across the theater, "**SHUT UP!!!!**"

Okay. Problem solved.

GGG's Lessons for Surviving Movies

❀ Trailers are cinematic propaganda that should be avoided like the plague.

❀ Take someone with you to the movies who is even more rude than the person yelling on her cell phone.

❀ If a movie is bad, try adding garlic and onions.

CHAPTER 19

RESUMES AND MARSHMALLOWS

Now that I had the SATs behind me, Mom insisted that I start drafting my resume while we waited for my scores to come back. Ugh. I had no idea what to put on there. I'd have my grades and SAT scores, and I had published a book, *The Grumpy Girl's Guide to Good Manners*. That was it—my resume was one quarter of an inch long. I started to panic, but then Mom assuaged my fears by reminding me that a lot of the things I had done during the tour promoting the aforementioned book counted as extracurricular activities, as did our travels to foreign countries.

I almost forgot about those! Woohoo!

So, I started recalling some of my experiences to cull the ones I could put on my resume.

When I was on tour in Florida, I did speak at a science museum where exactly *five* people showed up. Afterwards, I sat in the front lobby behind a table waiting to sign books. Anyway, a man showed up with a 12-year-old girl. He brought her to talk to me because she wanted to be a writer. She was a pretty girl and sweet, but for some reason this guy (her dad or uncle, I presume) told her in front of me and my mom that she lacked manners. And he was bringing her *to me* for help!?!?

Well, she started crying and I was mortified. At first, I pretended I didn't notice the only two people standing in front of my table in the empty front lobby of a science museum. When the girl walked away to cry behind a pillar, I got up to comfort her and said something to make her laugh.

That's good, right?!? I wonder how I can write that on my resume:

* **STOPPED 12-YEAR-OLD FROM CRYING AT A SCIENCE MUSEUM WHERE FIVE PEOPLE SHOWED UP TO HEAR ME TALK ABOUT MY BOOK**

or maybe

* **SURVIVED OVERSEAS TRIP WITH TWO SAFETY HAZARDS DISGUISED AS CHILDREN**

Sarah never had to rack her brain for ideas on what to put on her college resume. She had 20 million accomplishments. Mom even sent her to a resume-preparation camp in Arkansas so she could organize all her feats. (Who knew Arkansas was the resume-preparation capital of the world?) She went there right after she had gotten her wisdom teeth removed. Because she had some sort of weird reaction to the procedure, her face looked like someone with a nut allergy who had just eaten a barrel of peanuts. Much of the swelling had subsided by the time she had to go to Arkansas, but she was still poofy, as if she had giant marshmallows stuffed in her mouth. But she was Sarah, so

the guys thought, "Oooh—poofy cheeks, just how I like 'em!" and passed by all the other reasonably attractive, available, non-poofy-cheeked girls just to get to Sarah.

I wondered if Mom would send me to this camp, and if I went with marshmallows stuffed in my face, would the boys notice me. She didn't send me—so I never had the chance to find out.

I finally scrounged up enough things to fill up a page or two on my resume, and the resume compilation part of the college application ended successfully—finally it was time for a well-deserved break.

Just kidding, it didn't end there. Resumes are only part of the general admission tickets into the application process. You also need to send each university a specific application, recommendation letters, transcripts, as well as essays based on mysteriously boring questions. No, friends, this was only

the beginning…inning…<small>inning</small>…<small>inning</small>…<small>inning</small>….

Transcripts are a little like resumes, except even less fun. They are a compilation of the classes you took the four years of high school with your grades listed down the side. Most of my grades were homeschool grades, but I also had some from online courses that my mom made me take for a variety of teachers, plus some MWF school grades. My transcript was a quilt of homeschool, real school, and online school grades. It was a mess trying to find them all, since Mom had kept the documentation in various places. We spent several days poring over the contents of some brown filing boxes and trying to recall forgotten website passwords. Eventually, we found them all and drafted a transcript that was quasi-legible.

Finally, the transcript was done; I included a handful of items to put on my resume and I wrote the required essays. During this whole process, though, people were always giving me advice on where to apply to college. For example, one of my teachers from the MWF school suggested I go to Dallas Baptist University (DBU). He had gone there and said he had loved it, but that it was in the bad part of Dallas, out in a field.

I wondered if it was a good thing that he admitted it was in a dangerous area (because it proved him honest), or if it was so bad that he had no choice but to tell me to cover himself in case something happened to me there.

Our conversation continued:

He: *Also, it's next to a lake that is radioactive.*

Me: *A radioactive lake?*

He: *Yes, DBU is next to a radioactive lake, a power plant, a national cemetery and a huge church.*

Me: *I'm sure the church needs to be huge to push back against the powers of darkness.*

Actually, I had heard it's a pretty good school, and it might be even greater if I swam in the radioactive lake and got superpowers, but then there was the risk that my superpower might be the ability to read other people's thoughts—and people say enough bad things about me already, so I don't think it would be a good idea for me to know what they think, too.

Even though I planned to apply to 20 colleges, all of them pretentious—I mean, prestigious—and far away, I only sent out four applications, and all but one were close to home (but not to the college of the radioactive lake). I'm not sure why I didn't apply to many colleges; but it was more than Jeremy, who followed in Paul's footsteps and only applied to one college because it didn't require an essay.

Good thing he didn't find out about DBU, because he'd probably fall into the radioactive lake while sliding off the roof of his friend's car or something.

Oddly enough, none of the colleges I applied to required interviews, which was unfortunate because I had prepared an extensive list for them of non-Egyptian historical figures I wanted to meet.

GGG's Lessons for Surviving Building Your Resume

✿ Establish an escape plan in case a preteen starts crying during your book signing.

✿ Sisters make everything unfair.

✿ Always keep marshmallows on hand, just in case a cute boy walks by.

CHAPTER 20

COLLEGE, HERE I COME!

As I was waiting on responses from colleges, I still attended MWF school part-time, but by now I had a bad case of senioritis—the typical senior mentality of academic apocalypse. High school's ending soon, so there's no point in putting in any effort now. Why buy a new uniform just because this one is getting tight? Why start following the rules you failed to upkeep the last three and half years? Why brush your hair or teeth in the morning? Okay, maybe not those two. In any case, second-semester senior year of high school is the only time in life you can be justifiably smug and lackadaisical without reaping any long-term negative consequences.

In March of my senior year, I received a letter from one of the colleges I had applied to. It came in a big envelope—you know, huge and filled with lots of material—the kind that acceptance letters arrive in—and I was so excited, thinking they had accepted me. But when I opened it, it contained a bunch of pamphlets about the school with a letter that instructed, "Please Apply Now."

Then a week later, the dean of something or other at that same school sent me an email stating how impressed he was with my essay and to let him know if I had any questions. But still no acceptance letter. I was tempted to write him back and tell him if you like it then you should put a ring on it.

By the time the acceptance letters were trickling in, I had inexplicably decided I wanted to go to Texas Christian University (TCU), the college that is located 20 minutes from my hometown. Whaat??!! I know, I know. I had been so ready to get out of here and was really leaning toward the school that was far away, but I decided to stay near home. Who knows why. Maybe I wasn't finished inflicting my grumpiness on those nearest and dearest and I needed to complete my work.

Sometime in early April, I was slouching on the couch in my room, researching antidiuretic hormone deficiency for my anatomy assignment, when the little mailbox on my computer dinged. I opened the email—it was from TCU. I started reading lackadaisically until I got to "…is happy to offer Rachel Aboukhair a place at TCU this fall." I sat straight back up in my seat, as if the offer would be rescinded if I didn't have proper posture.

"Mom! Mommy! MAMA!"

I ran downstairs with my computer and showed Mom the email. I watched her face as she read it. She smiled at me and said, "Congratulations! Let's call Dad and Sarah!"

And that was it. Homescooling and high school were over. Well, not officially, but mentally I was done with them both. It's funny how the whole institute is preparation for this one thing—the acceptance letter—and now that I had gotten one, I had to move on to the next stage in my training as an Airbender—I mean, TCU Horned Frog—and then discern what the next stage was preparation for.

Mom called Dad first to tell him. Then, as she dialed Sarah's number, I asked her, "Okay, the point of high school is to get into college, so what's the point of college?"

She didn't hesitate. "To learn how to think, develop as a person, grow and mature, get a great education and eventually get a job."

"Genghis Khan didn't go to college, and he did all right!"

As previously mentioned, Mom only responds to my non-stupid comments.

"Sarah, guess what? Rachel got into TCU!"

I could hear Sarah on the other end of the line exclaim, "Really! Yay! I'm so excited for her!"

I got on the phone and Sarah asked me if I was excited and I said yes because I always thought that college was about building character in the face of adversity, expanding your horizons, and finding out who you are as you battle obstacles in the way of your passion. Just kidding. I didn't say any of that stuff. Besides, encountering more obstacles than I have already seemed highly improbable.

Mom got back on the line and talked to Sarah some more. As they conversed, I thought back on my life and school experiences thus far. I could see that neither had been typical. I wondered what my life would've been like if I had gone to a traditional school all the way through. Maybe then I would have had everything laid out for me, a clear path that I could have followed to get me to college. Instead, we pretty much blazed our own trail, and even though it wasn't conventional, it was certainly interesting. I've had to learn how to deal with people in foreign places, study different languages, cultures and customs, and figure out how to navigate life with two active brothers in tow. Those things alone have been an education in and of themselves. Once you add Hammurabi and Sophocles and Dostoyevsky to the mix, I feel like I might be able to survive freshman year at college.

While I was lost in reverie, Mom had put Sarah on speaker phone and said, "Rachel, the best part of starting college is that you won't know anybody, which will be a fresh start for you!"

Sarah jumped in, "Wait! She *will* know somebody! I heard Jason Kemp got into TCU as well!"

I froze and broke out in a cold sweat.

Well, so much for bew neginnings!

THE END

Acknowledgments

Thanks to Piero Rivolta, who took a chance with the *Grumpy Girl* and saw its possibilities.

Thanks to Ivana Lucic, president of New Chapter Publisher, for her tireless championing of the series.

Thanks to Chris Angermann, my editor. His keen eye and extensive experience contribute so much to the outcome.

Thanks to Vanessa Houston for her copy editing, fact-checking and excellent suggestions for improvement.

And finally, thanks to my mother for helping me and supporting me through the writing of this book.

About the Author

When Rachel's not imparting the joy that is her life to the world, she is a student at Texas Christian University (TCU). Please don't ask her what she's going to do after college—she doesn't know, and even if she did, she wouldn't tell you. When she is not doing schoolwork, Rachel doesn't really do very much. She doesn't have any dogs, cats or hobbies. But she is currently working on the next adventure in the *Grumpy Girl's Guide* series

For more information about
Rachel and her books
go to
www.thegrumpygirlsguide.com.

NOTES

If you haven't already read about Rachel's hilarious adventures
at a week-long etiquette camp
and her sardonic advice on rules for teenage behavior,
you're in for a treat!

It's available at

www.amazon,com

and

www.newchapterpublisher.com

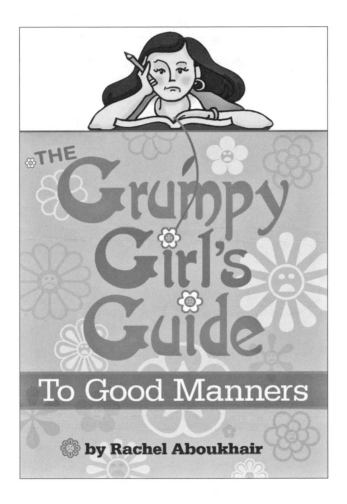

THE Grumpy Girl's Guide

To Good Manners

by Rachel Aboukhair